Flour Does Not Flower

Pam Scheunemann

Published by SandCastle™, an imprint of ABDO Publishing Company, 4940 Viking Drive, Edina, Minnesota 55435.

Printed in the United States.

Photo credits: Corbis Images, Comstock, Digital Vision, Eyewire Images, John Foxx Images, PhotoDisc, Rubberball Productions

Library of Congress Cataloging-in-Publication Data

Scheunemann, Pam, 1955–
    Flour does not flower / Pam Scheunemann.
        p. cm. -- (Homophones)
    Includes index.
    Summary: Photographs and simple text introduce homophones, words that sound alike but are spelled differently and have different meanings.
    ISBN 1-57765-742-X (hardcover)
    ISBN 1-59197-063-6 (paperback)
    1. English language--Homonyms--Juvenile literature. [1. English language--Homonyms.] I. Title. II. Series.

PE1595 .S34 2002
428.1--dc21

                                                                    2001053326

The SandCastle concept, content, and reading method have been reviewed and approved by a national advisory board including literacy specialists, librarians, elementary school teachers, early childhood education professionals, and parents.

Let Us Know

After reading the book, SandCastle would like you to tell us your stories about reading. What is your favorite page? Was there something hard that you needed help with? Share the ups and downs of learning to read. We want to hear from you! To get posted on the ABDO Publishing Company Web site, send us email at:

sandcastle@abdopub.com

About SandCastle™

A professional team of educators, reading specialists, and content developers created the SandCastle™ series to support young readers as they develop reading skills and strategies and increase their general knowledge. The SandCastle™ series has four levels that correspond to early literacy development in young children. The levels are provided to help teachers and parents select the appropriate books for young readers.

Emerging Readers
(no flags)

Beginning Readers
(1 flag)

Transitional Readers
(2 flags)

Fluent Readers
(3 flags)

These levels are meant only as a guide. All levels are subject to change.

To see a complete list of SandCastle™ books and other nonfiction titles from ABDO Publishing Company, visit www.abdopub.com or contact us at:
4940 Viking Drive, Edina, Minnesota 55435 • 1-800-800-1312 • fax: 1-952-831-1632

fairy

ferry

Homophones are words that sound alike but are spelled differently and have different meanings.

Fir trees are green.

A kitten has soft fur.

We went **for** a swim.

There are four of us.

We like to **find** shells.

You get fined for late movies.

Spot does not have fleas.

Tony **flees** from the bull.

The gull flew very high.

Mom has the flu.

A rooster is a fowl.

Ron hit a foul ball.

Our feet are raised high.

Winning was quite a feat.

Jerry paid the cab fare.

Where are these people?
(the fair)

Words I Can Read

Nouns

A noun is a person, place, or thing

foul ball (FOUL BAWL) p. 17

bull (BULL) p. 13

fair (FAIR) p. 21

fairy (FAIR-ee) p. 4

fare (FAIR) p. 20

feat (FEET) p. 19

feet (FEET) p. 18

ferry (FER-ee) p. 4

fir trees (FUR TREEZ) p. 6

fleas (FLEEZ) p. 12

flu (FLOO) p. 15

fowl (FOUL) p. 16

fur (FUR) p. 7

gull (GUHL) p. 14

homophones (HOME-uh-fonez) p. 5

kitten (KIT-uhn) p. 7

meanings (MEE-ningz) p. 5

movies (MOO-veez) p. 11

people (PEE-puhl) p. 21

rooster (ROO-stur) p. 16

shells (SHELZ) p. 10

swim (SWIM) p. 8

winnings (WIN-ing) p. 19

words (WURDZ) p. 5

Proper Nouns

A proper noun is the name
of a person, place, or thing

Jerry (JER-ee) p. 20

Mom (MOM) p. 15

Ron (RON) p. 17

Spot (SPOT) p. 12

Tony (TOH-nee) p. 13

Verbs

A verb is an action or being word

are (AR)
    pp. 5, 6, 9, 18, 21

does (DUHZ) p. 12

find (FINDE) p. 10

fined (FINDE) p. 11

flees (FLEEZ) p. 13

flew (FLOO) p. 14

get (GET) p. 11

has (HAZ) pp. 7, 15

have (HAV) pp. 5, 12

hit (HIT) p. 17

is (IZ) p. 16

like (LIKE) p. 10

paid (PAYD) p. 20

raised (RAYZD) p. 18

sound (SOUND) p. 5

spelled (SPELD) p. 5

was (WUHZ) p. 19

went (WENT) p. 8

Picture Words

fir

fur

flower

flour